420
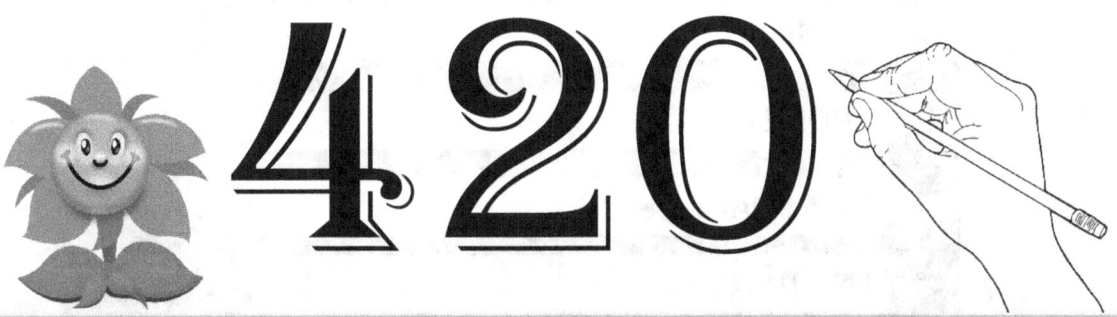

TRIPPY THINGS TO DRAW WHILE HIGH

All rights reserved. No part of this book may be reproduced in any form by any electronic or mechanical means including photocopying, recording, or information storage and retrieval without permission in writing from the author.

© Copyright 2021

By Jason R. Moore

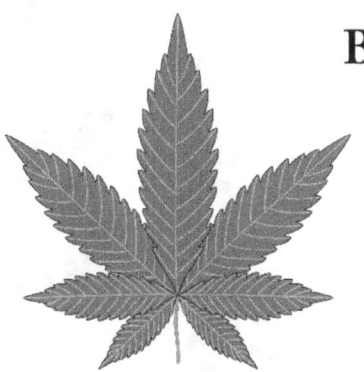

IF FOUND, PLEASE CALL: OR VISIT:

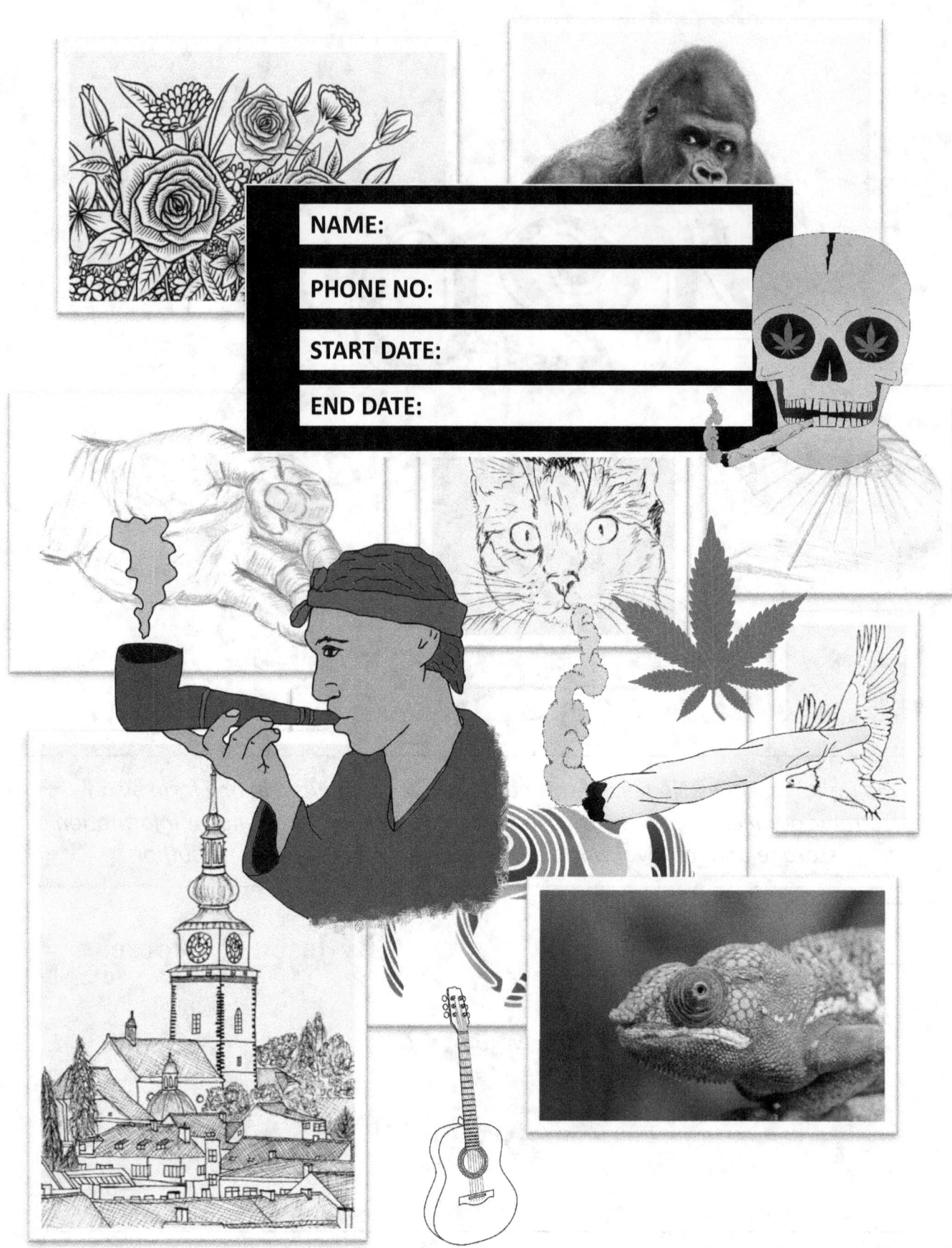

420 TRIPPY DRAWING IDEAS FOR STONERS (Things to Draw While High)

Are you a stoner looking for WeedSpirational Drawing Ideas? Or you need the perfect gift for a marijuana lover?

Then this book is just what you need!

This book is jam-packed with 420 CREATIVE TRIPPY DRAWING IDEAS & PROJECTS which you can use daily. For each day, you will find an exciting drawing challenge, with tips and brief explanation for every challenge.

With this book, you will never run out of ideas!

All rights reserved. No part of this book may be reproduced in any form by any electronic or mechanical means including photocopying, recording, or information storage and retrieval without permission in writing from the author.

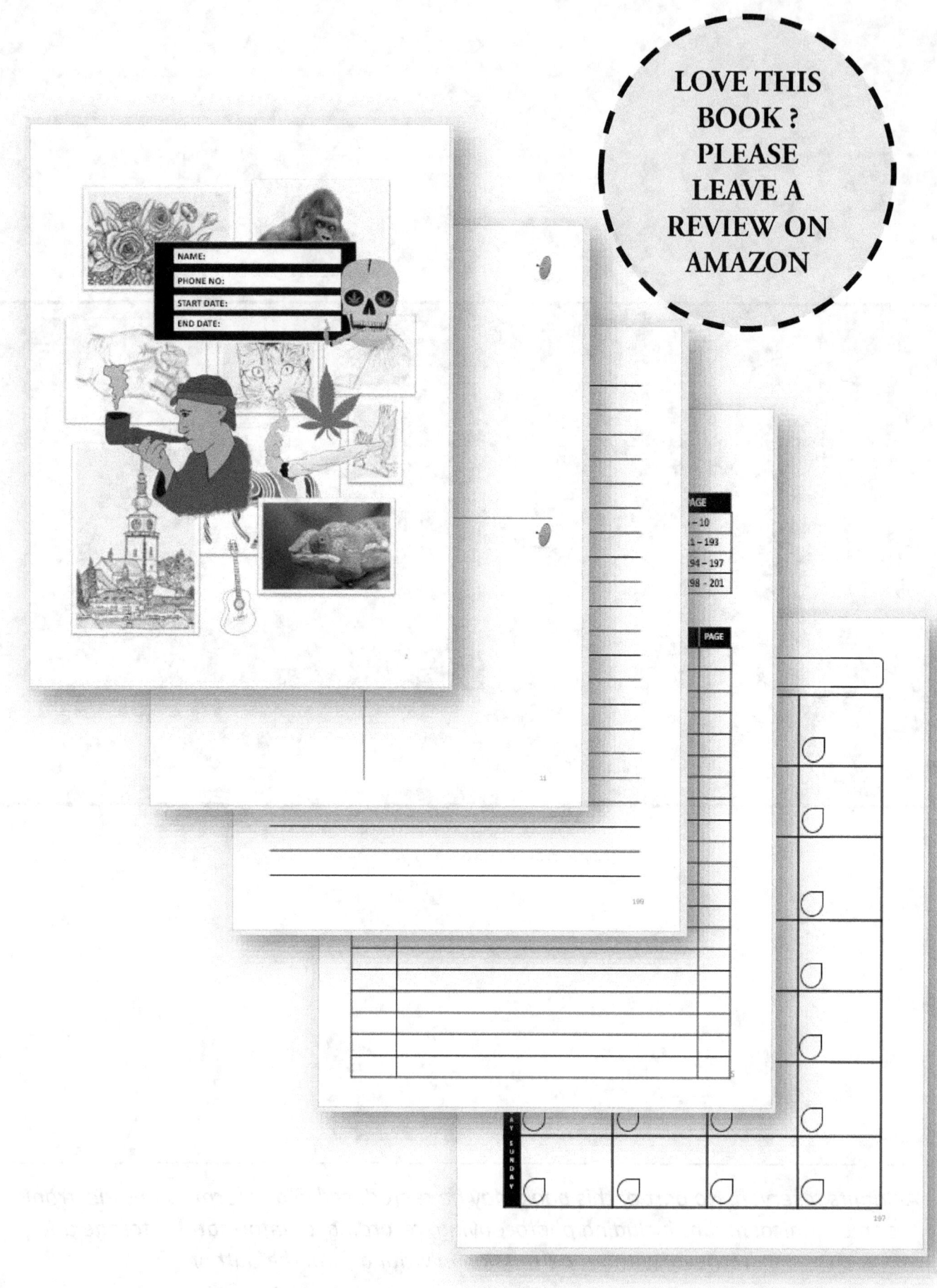

LOVE THIS BOOK ? PLEASE LEAVE A REVIEW ON AMAZON

TABLE OF CONTENTS

TITLE	PAGE
INDEX	5 – 10
420 TRIPPY THINGS TO DRAW WHILE HIGH	11 – 115
UNDATED CALENDAR	116 – 127
NOTES SECTION	128 - 131

FAVORITE DRAWINGS

DATE	TITLE	PAGE

FAVORITE DRAWINGS

DATE	TITLE	PAGE

FAVORITE DRAWINGS

DATE	TITLE	PAGE

FAVORITE DRAWINGS

DATE	TITLE	PAGE

FAVORITE DRAWINGS

DATE	TITLE	PAGE

FAVORITE DRAWINGS

DATE	TITLE	PAGE

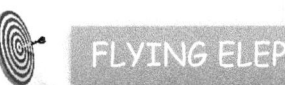 FLYING ELEPHANT

 HANDS AS LEGS, LEGS AS HANDS

 PLEADING CHICKEN

 MILKY WAY

SMOKING SKELETON

HUMAN BRIDGE

 SMILING CUP

 MANSION

RABBIT LAYING EGGS

STONERS SHRINE

EVOLUTION

COBRA

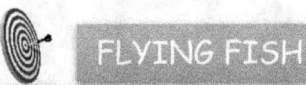 FLYING FISH

 SINGING COW

 RIVER IN THE MOON

 CRAB

HURRICAIN ON WEED AS SMOKE | PATHWAY TO HIGHNESS

 OPPOSITE | 5 LADY BUGS

GANJA FACTORY

WOLF GOAT

 HAMBURGER

BALCONY

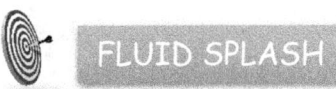 FLUID SPLASH

SEA URCHIN

 SWORD

BARN

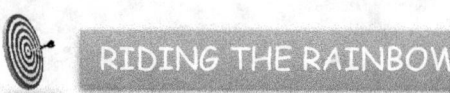 RIDING THE RAINBOW

 WEED KING

 AMULET

 ARROW GANJA

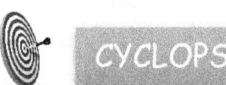 CYCLOPS

 SHOCKER

 SILENT MORNING

 HIGH STATUE

ANGRY MOON

 STAYING TRIPPY

 DYING CAR

 GRAVEYARD

FISHING TREE

 ON MASK

 SNAKE WOMAN

 CHILDHOOD

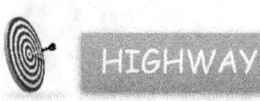 HIGHWAY

 STONED COW

 ADMIRATION

 BRAINY

WEED ON BINOCULAR | GUN

 NAILS | NEW INVENTION

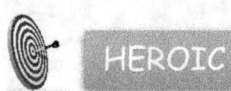 HEROIC

 TELEPHONE

 FAVORITE PET

 BABY IN LANTERN

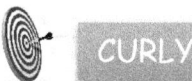 CURLY

 HELPING

 MODELING

 FROZEN

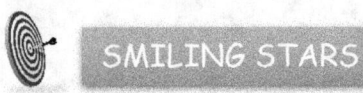 SMILING STARS

 HIGH VIBES

 UNBALANCED LIFE

 BUGS

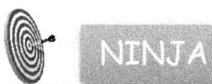 NINJA

SOBER TREE

 WEED CORN

BULLET

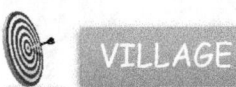 VILLAGE

 LETTER WEED

 PUFF PUFF

 TRADITIONAL CLOTH

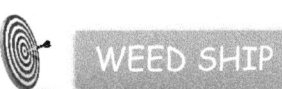 WEED SHIP	SMOKING SAND
PATHWAYS	BOW AND ARROW

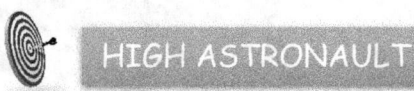 **HIGH ASTRONAULT**   **FOREVER YOURS**

 EVERYTHING HIGH   **ARMOR**

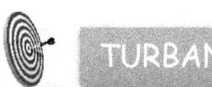 TURBAN

 FLEA

 SNAKE WEED

 PIE

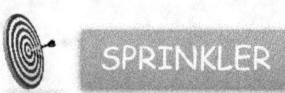 SPRINKLER

 HIGH CAT

 SMASHED

 HAIR WEED

PENCIL WITH LEAVES

SQUIRREL NINJA

 CAKE SLICE

FLOWER POT

33

DOGS OF FLOWERS	WHALE
DOG FISH	GOGGLES ON EGG

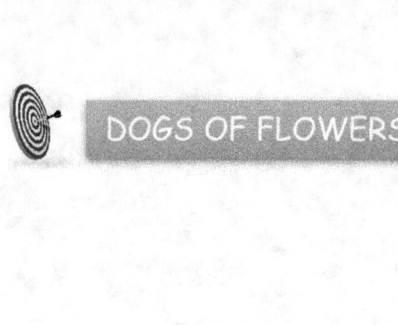

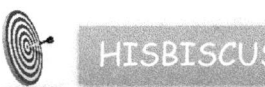 HISBISCUS

CRYING MOON

 CATHEDRAL

CRYING BOMB

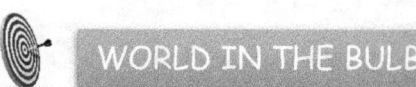 WORLD IN THE BULB

 WOMEN MADE OF BUTTERFLY

 HIGH PANDA

 SOMETHING YOU MISS

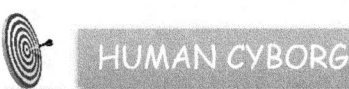 HUMAN CYBORG

WEED IN JAIL

 VINYL

FERRY

BULL	POPCORN
MADE OF NUMBERS	CRANE

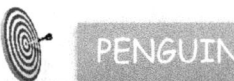 PENGUIN

THROWBACK

 WHAT INSPIRES YOU

PIANO

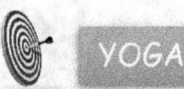 YOGA RAT

PIZZA

 WATER MELON

CRICKET

MAN CARRYING HIS HEAD

 GOODBYE

 WARRIOR

 ICICLES

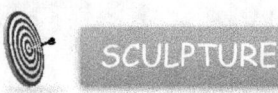 SCULPTURE

 EAGLE TORTOISE

HOT POTATOE

WEED STORE

WOMAN WITH 7 EYES RECIPE

 MUSHROOM WITH BIG ROOT PALACE

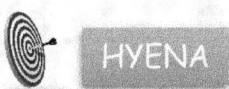 HYENA

 VINTAGE OBJECT

 KIWI GIANT

 LEAVES WITH HEAD

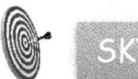 SKY

DONUT

 LABORATORY MUSHROOMS

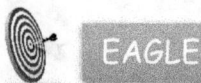 **EAGLE**

 TOURISM SITE

 BIRD CAMP

 BIRDY TREE

LEVITATING STONER | **PARROT**

 MIDNIGHT PARTY | **HOT DOG**

DROWNING, STILL SMOKING | LOBSTER

 OH, MY LASY GANJA | BUTTERFLY

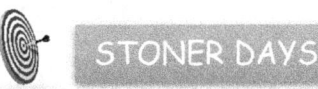 STONER DAYS

 SMOKING WITH EYES

 IMPALA

 WOLF

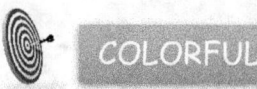 COLORFUL

 TREES

 TUTRTLE

 VILLIAN

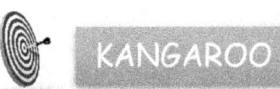 KANGAROO

 OSTRICH

 TREE HOUSE

 CUTLERY

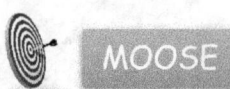 MOOSE   UNDERWORLD

 HELP ROBOT   FRENCH FRIES

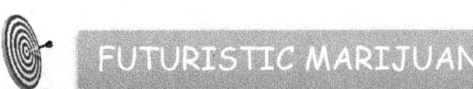 FUTURISTIC MARIJUANA

REINDEER

 MOTH

PATHWAY

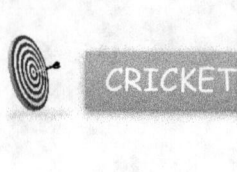 CRICKET

BAT

 BADGER

REGRET

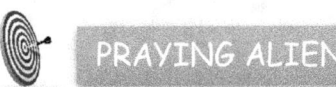 PRAYING ALIEN

 SMILING WEED

 TIGER

 PERIWINKLE

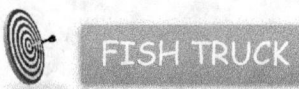 **FISH TRUCK**

BUILDING PLAN

 MAGICAL WORLD

RAVEN

BOUQUET

 MUSHROOM FINGERS

 WEED MUNTAIN

 JELLY FISH

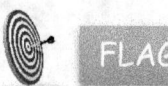 **FLAG**

 LIGHTNING

VAMPIRES **SEEING THINGS**

STONER BEAR

 DRAGON LION

 RED WHALE

 WEED DOCTORS

TABLE	INVERTED
SHRINE	PIRATES

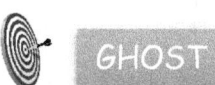 GHOST

WEED BEARD

 SWEETHEARTS

CAMEL

RIVER IN A CAMERA

WEED BUBBLES

 STONER COUPLES

FIGHTING FINGERS

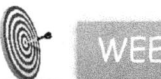 WEED LOGO

 STYLISH ANT

 SEA LION

 WEIRD GATE

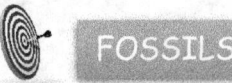 FOSSILS

 STARVATION

 ELEPHANT

 REGRET

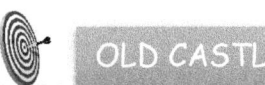 OLD CASTLE

 HURRCAIN

 DRUMMING HEAD

 COYOTE

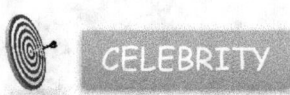 CELEBRITY

 MAST

 SKY

 INSIDE THE HOUSE

YOU AS THE OPPOSITE GENDER

GUITAR

 TREE FROM AXE

BULB WITH A ROOM

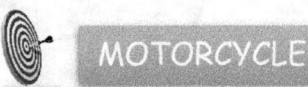 MOTORCYCLE

COURT

 SNOWMAN

MOUNTAIN CUT INTO THREE

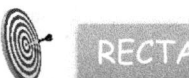 RECTANGLE PLANTS

 BREEZY FEELING

 CAKE SLICE

 MAN POOL

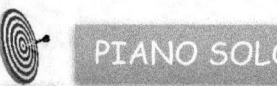 PIANO SOLO | FRIDGE

 GAME CONSOLE | LEAVES WITH HEAD

EYES IN THE EYEBALL

GHOST THE SAND

 UNDERWATER WORLD

FUTURE TRANSPORTAION MEANS

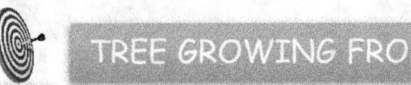 TREE GROWING FROM HANDS | LOSING DAYLIGHT

 BEST SMOKER | FLOWERS GROWING FROM DEER HORN

CRAZY AFTERNOON

 ROAD ENTERING THE SUN

 BULB WITH A ROOT

 TREE ON GIRAFFE

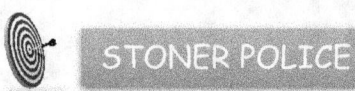 STONER POLICE

CRYING BEE

 PLANET MEETING

GOAT WITH WINGS

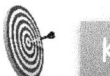 KNIFE

 JUMPING

 BABY WITH WEED

 AQUARIUM

SLAVE QUEEN

PIANO WITH STRINGS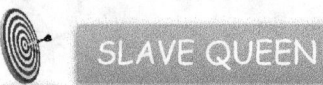

 ORANGE

FOREST

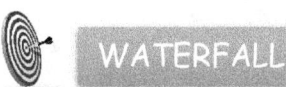 WATERFALL | WREATH

 ZUCCHINI | ON VACATION

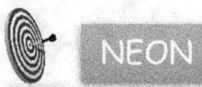 NEON

MUMMY STONER

 TATTOO

ROLLING WHELL

SMOKING POT

LOUSE

 SQUID

HANGING WEED

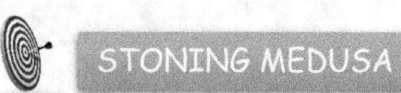 STONING MEDUSA

 WORKING OUT WITH GANJA

 GRASSHOPPER

 THERMOS

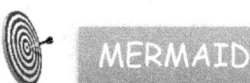 MERMAID

REJECTION

 ANCIENT PEOPLE

BUDDY GANJA

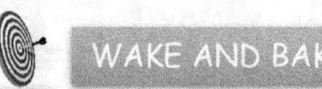 WAKE AND BAKE UP

DRUNK CLOUD

 SLEEPING ON WEED BED

LAUGHING SCOOTER

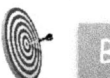 BERBEQUE

 CENTEPEDE

 STONER SNAKE

 WALKING SNAKE

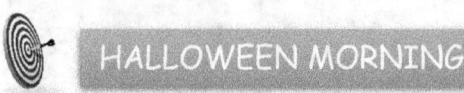 HALLOWEEN MORNING

PASTRY

 WITCH HOUSE

WEED HEAD

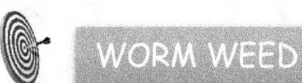 WORM WEED

 WEED FINGERS

 FURIOUS

 LOUD WEED

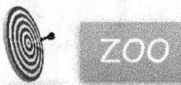 ZOO

 STONER UNICORN

 CAN FOOD

 DATING WEED

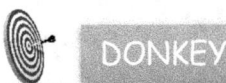 DONKEY

HAPPY MONSTER

 FISH

FLAMINGO

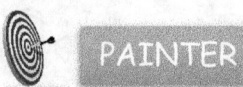 PAINTER
 CATERPILLAR
 CHAMELEON
 SHORT COMIC

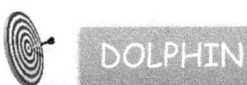 DOLPHIN

RAT LIFTING WEIGHT

CAT NAME STONER

UMBRELLA

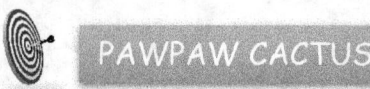 PAWPAW CACTUS

BEAUTIFUL CELESTIAL

 BURNING HOUSE

DESERTED HIGHLAND

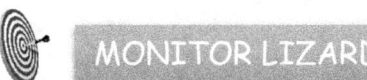 MONITOR LIZARD

NEVER GIVE UP

 DOLL HOUSE

ROLLERCOASTER

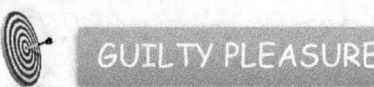 **GUILTY PLEASURE**

 ZODIAC

 FATHER STONER

 CHRISTMAS WEED

MUSIC NOTES

FRIENDSHIP

 RADIO

BASKETBALLER

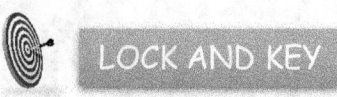 LOCK AND KEY

SHRUBS

 PHOTOGRAPHER

WOODPECKER

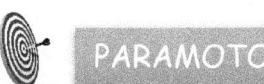 PARAMOTORIST

PUZZLE

 BABOON

APE

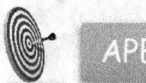 APE

 CAMPING WEEDERS

 SUPERHERO DOCTOR

 ATHLETE

 FRYER

 GANJA PLAYING SAXOPHONE

 HELICOPTER

 SMOKERS COUNTRY

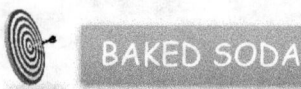 BAKED SODA

 CHESS BOARD

 MARIJUANA PLAYING BALL

 LAUGHING AND CRYING

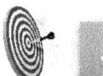 SMOKING FINGERS | WEED GUITAR

 EATING SHOVEL | CHAMELEON TURNING WEED

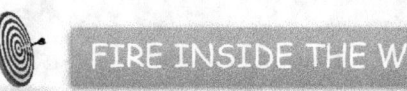 FIRE INSIDE THE WELL

 WEED ON PAGEANTRY

 SMOKING SMOKE

 EATING EYES

SQUIRELL SMOKING ITS TAIL

BANANA RING

 WEED PLAYING GUITAR

VERY OLD WEEDER

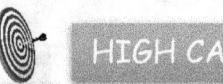 HIGH CAT

 THE THINNER THE BETTER

 WEED ON MOTOBIKE

 SCREAMING EYE

QUEEN

 HURRICAIN

 BUTTERFLY INSIDE BULB

 GHOST

STONER WAR	WORM
WITHOUT WORRY	WITCH CRAFT

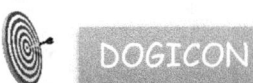 DOGICON   DREAM HOUSE

 KING   DESKTOP

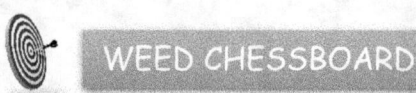 WEED CHESSBOARD

EAGLE

 BEARDY

HALF HUMAN, HALF ALIEN

EYES IN THE PALM

 WORLD ON THE PALM

 FLUFFY

 BLITZED DRUG

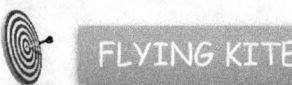 FLYING KITE

 THE WORLD WITH NOSE MASK

 TREE GROWING ON LEAVES

 GRADUATING DOGS

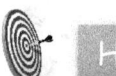 HOLDING GANJA CAREFULLY

SHOCKED

 TAP WATER

WEED QUEEN

ROCKSTAR	FOX
HIGH MUSIC	TOASTY EYES

RIDING THE RAINBOW

 WEED PROSON

 FROZEN

 HAMMER GOD

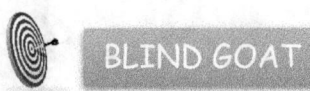 BLIND GOAT

 DIAMOND

 GIFT BOX

CUTTING OFF AN EXPOLSION SMOKE

SECRET PLACE OF THE MOST HIGH | **ANNOYED GANJA**

 GANJA LION | **STORMY CANNABIS**

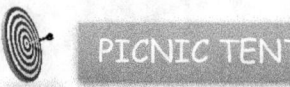 PICNIC TENT

 SHOE CANOE

 CLOCK ON EGG

 SMOKING SUN

COLORFUL CANNABIS | COMPASS

 FIGHTING SHADOWS | WEED PYRAMID

MONTH:		**YEAR:**		**GOAL:**

MONDAY	◯	◯	◯	◯
TUESDAY	◯	◯	◯	◯
WEDNESDAY	◯	◯	◯	◯
THURSDAY	◯	◯	◯	◯
FRIDAY	◯	◯	◯	◯
SATURDAY	◯	◯	◯	◯
SUNDAY	◯	◯	◯	◯

| MONTH: | YEAR: | GOAL: |

MONDAY	⬤	⬤	⬤	⬤
TUESDAY	⬤	⬤	⬤	⬤
WEDNESDAY	⬤	⬤	⬤	⬤
THURSDAY	⬤	⬤	⬤	⬤
FRIDAY	⬤	⬤	⬤	⬤
SATURDAY	⬤	⬤	⬤	⬤
SUNDAY	⬤	⬤	⬤	⬤

	MONTH:	YEAR:	GOAL:
MONDAY	⟿	⟿	⟿	⟿
TUESDAY	⟿	⟿	⟿	⟿
WEDNESDAY	⟿	⟿	⟿	⟿
THURSDAY	⟿	⟿	⟿	⟿
FRIDAY	⟿	⟿	⟿	⟿
SATURDAY	⟿	⟿	⟿	⟿
SUNDAY	⟿	⟿	⟿	⟿

MONTH:	YEAR:	GOAL:

MONDAY				
TUESDAY				
WEDNESDAY				
THURSDAY				
FRIDAY				
SATURDAY				
SUNDAY				

MONTH: **YEAR:** **GOAL:**

MONDAY	◯	◯	◯	◯
TUESDAY	◯	◯	◯	◯
WEDNESDAY	◯	◯	◯	◯
THURSDAY	◯	◯	◯	◯
FRIDAY	◯	◯	◯	◯
SATURDAY	◯	◯	◯	◯
SUNDAY	◯	◯	◯	◯

| MONTH: | YEAR: | GOAL: |

MONDAY	⬯	⬯	⬯	⬯
TUESDAY	⬯	⬯	⬯	⬯
WEDNESDAY	⬯	⬯	⬯	⬯
THURSDAY	⬯	⬯	⬯	⬯
FRIDAY	⬯	⬯	⬯	⬯
SATURDAY	⬯	⬯	⬯	⬯
SUNDAY	⬯	⬯	⬯	⬯

MONTH: **YEAR:** **GOAL:**

MONDAY				
TUESDAY				
WEDNESDAY				
THURSDAY				
FRIDAY				
SATURDAY				
SUNDAY				

| MONTH: | YEAR: | GOAL: |

MONDAY				
TUESDAY				
WEDNESDAY				
THURSDAY				
FRIDAY				
SATURDAY				
SUNDAY				

| MONTH: | YEAR: | GOAL: |

MONDAY				
TUESDAY				
WEDNESDAY				
THURSDAY				
FRIDAY				
SATURDAY				
SUNDAY				

| MONTH: | YEAR: | GOAL: |

MONDAY				
TUESDAY				
WEDNESDAY				
THURSDAY				
FRIDAY				
SATURDAY				
SUNDAY				

| | MONTH: | YEAR: | GOAL: |

MONDAY	⬗	⬗	⬗	⬗
TUESDAY	⬗	⬗	⬗	⬗
WEDNESDAY	⬗	⬗	⬗	⬗
THURSDAY	⬗	⬗	⬗	⬗
FRIDAY	⬗	⬗	⬗	⬗
SATURDAY	⬗	⬗	⬗	⬗
SUNDAY	⬗	⬗	⬗	⬗

| MONTH: | YEAR: | GOAL: |

MONDAY	◯	◯	◯	◯
TUESDAY	◯	◯	◯	◯
WEDNESDAY	◯	◯	◯	◯
THURSDAY	◯	◯	◯	◯
FRIDAY	◯	◯	◯	◯
SATURDAY	◯	◯	◯	◯
SUNDAY	◯	◯	◯	◯

www.ingramcontent.com/pod-product-compliance
Lightning Source LLC
Chambersburg PA
CBHW060418220526
45465CB00008B/2937